CHANGE THE STORY

CHANGE THE STORY

A GUIDED JOURNAL
FOR INSPIRING AWARENESS
AND ACTION TODAY AND BEYOND

Kristine Pidkameny

CICO BOOKS
LONDON NEW YORK

Published in 2020 by CICO Books
An imprint of Ryland Peters & Small Ltd
20–21 Jockey's Fields, London WC1R 4BW
341 E 116th St, New York, NY 10029

www.rylandpeters.com

10 9 8 7 6 5 4 3 2 1

A CIP catalog record for this book is available from the
Library of Congress and the British Library.

Hardback ISBN: 978-1-78249-923-7
Paperback ISBN: 978-1-80065-024-4

Printed in China

Senior editor: Carmel Edmonds
Senior designer: Emily Breen
Art director: Sally Powell
Head of production: Patricia Harrington
Publishing manager: Penny Craig
Publisher: Cindy Richards

CONTENTS

INTRODUCTION

How we grow, expand, and evolve throughout our lives is a deeply personal experience. So is keeping a journal that records these experiences. Small steps and shifts along the way lead to bigger changes, both in life and on the written page. Your journey is your story and identifying the key turning points in your story can be life-changing, for both you and the greater community.

This interactive journal for self-reflection and transformation is filled with guidance and plenty of writing space to explore your hopes and dreams and go beyond the written page to take positive action. What causes are you most passionate about? How can you share your vision with others? Whether it is volunteering at a food bank or campaigning about climate change, there are many ways to be the proactive change you want to see and to inspire others.

Each prompt will encourage you to look differently at your life, other people, and everyday situations, and define the areas in your life that are essential for you to focus your energy toward. If you are not doing that as much as you'd like, you can explore how to better prioritize your activities and schedule. Journaling benefits your well-being and mental health and can also be a powerful tool to help you become an effective leader. Through reflecting on your ideas, experiences, and skills, you gain perspective. In turn this can guide you to making better decisions. Choose to own your story and bring its purpose and value out into the world. You can make a difference.

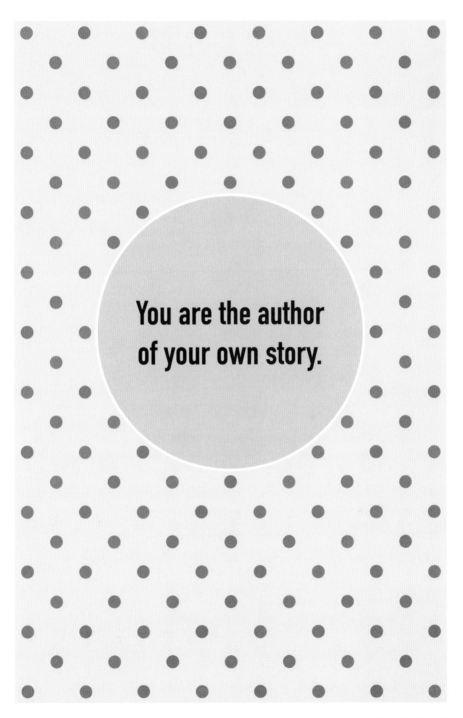

You are the author
of your own story.

PAVE A NEW WAY

There are six sections in the guided journal. Within each section you will find
a wide range of writing prompts, activities, and meditations to inspire and
encourage your journey of self-empowerment. For maximum benefit follow
the sections in order, as each one builds on the one before.

EVERY WORD OPENS A DOORWAY

We begin with some warm-up writing prompts to explore the power of words to
awaken our awareness. Whether written or spoken, there is great value in
examining and paying close attention to the energy and intent of our words.

RECONNECT WITH YOUR AUTHENTIC SELF

Before stepping out into the world to take action, it is key to know yourself better.
Here we take a look at your past, present, and future. Whose eyes and what lens
are you looking through in these experiences? Be honest. What have you learned
so far? What do you want in life and what steps will you take to get there?
Investigating and accepting our imperfections, fears, and uncertainties allows us
to find the courage and curiosity to step forward and become clear about what is
important to us. It matters to feel at home in your personal story.

DARE TO DREAM

After a close look at your inner landscape, the next step is to expand and explore
your ideas even further. Be inspired as you imagine the future and reimagine your
life there—the people, dreams, and causes you are passionate about. What if I did
this or met so and so? What would happen if I took this action or risk? Become
more discerning in your decisions, both present and future, and direct your
energies in the best way to do what you love and make a difference in the world.

TAKE THE DEEP DIVE

Are you in? Now it's time to take the actual steps and risks to bring your story and vision out into the world. Here's where your ideas and journaling get real, including more specific time lines for taking action and embracing unknown opportunities. Being new at something is uncomfortable. Get comfortable being uncomfortable and not knowing. You are testing the waters and moving closer toward sharing your personal vision with others.

SAY YES TO YOUR BEST SELF

Owning your story and bringing your vision out into the world is empowering and uplifting. These positive actions can actually be a part of your self-care. On the flip side, if there are times you notice they use up too much of your energy, perhaps even before you realize it, that can be a cause for concern. It's important to consider the balance of your total wellness—mind, body, and heart—to see how all these aspects together benefit and support your larger purpose.

BE THE CHANGE AND REMAIN INSPIRED

You've got this. What you focus your attention on and what you practice grows stronger. In this final section you monitor your activities, commitments, and challenges, and keep yourself motivated in the present and moving forward. As you continue to show up and be the proactive change you want to see around you, you inspire others. How are you turning obstacles into opportunities? How do you speak through your life? You choose to be the one to change the conversation in the room. You believe you can do it—and you do it.

WRITING TIPS AND HELPFUL HABITS

As you carve out the time to write and make space for your dreams, consistency is important. Commit to doing something every day, however small, including the days when you'd rather not show up. Whether you're new to journal writing or have been at it for a while, the motivation to get started and the encouragement to keep at it are essential. Helpful habits and feeling supported go a long way.

Incorporate journal writing into your daily routine. Figure out what works best for your individual lifestyle.

•

Set clear boundaries for your dedicated time to journal. It will help you stay on track when your initial motivation and excitement fades. To be more accountable, you may choose to find a journal writing buddy for check-ins and setting goals.

•

Make your journal writing experience something you look forward to. Find a favorable location where you're able to focus. The space may be indoors or outdoors, private or public.

•

Appeal to your senses and come up with a cue that invites comfort while journaling. Maybe have a favorite pillow, plant, or vase of flowers nearby while you write, or wear a favorite article of clothing or your lucky hat.

•

Rituals can be grounding and reinforce showing up to write every day. Create a signal for beginning and ending your journal writing session—perhaps lighting a candle, drinking a favorite beverage, or using a particular writing implement. Make it something personal.

•

Remember to take a breather as needed. Rest is important and so is self-compassion, especially at any low points or when you have setbacks. They're all part of the journey.

•

Part of the journey, too, is joy and gratitude. Acknowledge your progress. Take the time to celebrate your small accomplishments along the way. They all add up.

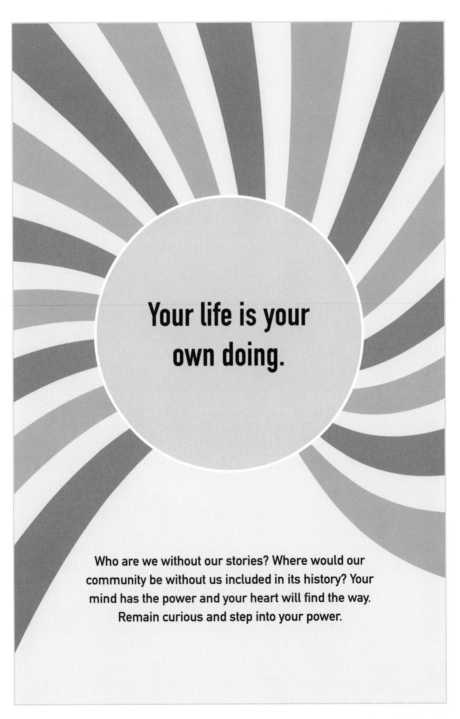

Your life is your own doing.

Who are we without our stories? Where would our community be without us included in its history? Your mind has the power and your heart will find the way. Remain curious and step into your power.

1

EVERY WORD
OPENS
A DOORWAY

Discover the power of words

to ignite awareness

Today's the start of your life-changing story. Set a timer for five minutes and write a message to yourself. How does this first step feel—any expectations, curiosities, particular goals, doubts, fears, inspirations? Your choice. This is for your eyes only. Feel free to write about whatever comes up.

Create a personal A-Z alphabet of awareness.
Assign to each letter of the alphabet a descriptive
word that conveys energy and expansion for you.
For example, A = allow; B = believe.

A ....   N ....

B ....   O ....

C ....   P ....

D ....   Q ....

E ....   R ....

F ....   S ....

G ....   T ....

H ....   U ....

I ....   V ....

J ....   W ....

K ....   X ....

L ....   Y ....

M ....   Z ....

Set a timer for five minutes and write down all the empowering
and uplifting words that come to mind immediately.

_____

Use a dictionary and write down additional empowering and
uplifting words that weren't included on your above list.

_____

Identify key words and phrases you notice yourself favoring
in conversations and writing.

_____

Review the above. Do they convey self-empowerment?
Revise any words or phrases accordingly.

_____

List ten words that express how you feel in this moment while writing. Compose a few sentences using these words.

---

1 _____   6 _____

2 _____   7 _____

3 _____   8 _____

4 _____   9 _____

5 _____   10 _____

_____

_____

_____

_____

_____

List ten words that describe how you imagine tomorrow to be. Compose a few sentences using these words.

---

1 _____   6 _____

2 _____   7 _____

3 _____   8 _____

4 _____   9 _____

5 _____   10 _____

_____

_____

_____

_____

_____

What words best portray the role of a leader?
Use them in a sentence.

What words best portray the role of a follower?
Use them in a sentence.

Make a list of words that convey traditional "negative"
qualities about yourself.

_____

_____

_____

_____

_____

_____

_____

_____

Review the above and consider if these qualities can be
reframed positively.

_____

_____

_____

_____

_____

_____

_____

_____

TIP

**Many "negative" qualities are in fact points of strength.
For example, stubborn = strong-minded;
hesitant = takes time to think things over.**

"There is a stubbornness about me that never can bear to be frightened at the will of others. My courage always rises at every attempt to intimidate me."

Jane Austen

Create a collage of words that illustrate the unique challenges
you have faced in life.

Create a collage of inspirational words describing the
principles that will guide your future vision of yourself.

_____

Create a list of associations for the following words:

Community

_____

_____

_____

Vision

_____

_____

_____

Activism

_____

_____

_____

Self-care

_____

_____

_____

Connection

_____

_____

_____

Passion

_____

_____

_____

Work

_____

_____

_____

Generosity

_____

_____

_____

Joy

_____

_____

_____

Beginnings

_____

_____

_____

Choose three words that give a vivid account of a
life-changing moment you have already experienced
and use these words in one sentence.

1

2

3

Choose three motivating words to express a life-change
you envision in your future and create a positive personal
motto including these words.

1

2

3

NEXT STEP

To feel even more empowered, read your motto aloud.

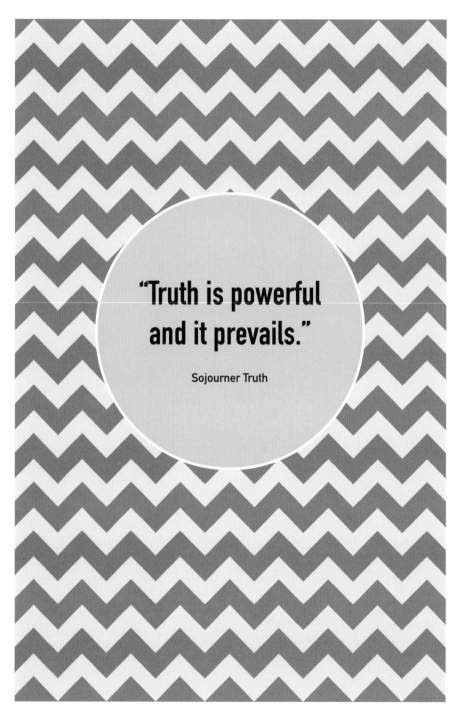

"Truth is powerful and it prevails."

Sojourner Truth

If you could leave a message to the world in a time capsule that others will read in the future, what would it say?

2

RECONNECT WITH YOUR AUTHENTIC SELF

Explore both past and present to remember who you truly are

As a child, what did you dream of becoming and doing
when you grew up?

_____

What was your favorite subject in school and do you
still have the same interest?

_____

Who was your favorite superhero growing up and why?

_____

What was your favorite book or movie as a child and why?

_____

What life stories from your past do you retell over and over in conversations with others or within your own thoughts?

Review the previous page. Do these life stories support your present or keep you stuck in the past? Why?

Describe a vulnerable time in your life in which you faced
the challenge of a "first time" experience and what you
learned from it.

_____

_____
_____
_____
_____
_____
_____
_____
_____
_____
_____

List other significant lessons you have learned in
your life so far.

_____

_____
_____
_____
_____
_____
_____
_____
_____
_____
_____
_____

List any nicknames people have called you in the past,
or perhaps still do. Were they appropriate for how you saw
yourself in the past? How you see yourself now?

_____

Who from your past has had the greatest impact on
your life and why?

_____

Write a letter to your younger self including any guidance or
support you feel would have been helpful at the time.

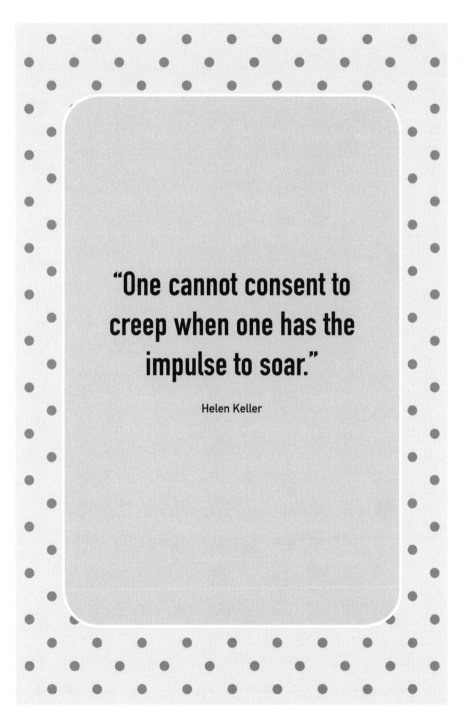

"One cannot consent to creep when one has the impulse to soar."

Helen Keller

What makes your heart sing and brings a smile to your face?

How would you like to be pleasantly surprised?

What do you care most deeply about? What energizes you?

_____

_____

_____

_____

_____

_____

_____

_____

_____

_____

Watch where your energy goes throughout the day—at different locations, people you interact with, activities you engage with, thoughts. Notice any patterns? Which ones are beneficial, and which are ones you'd like to improve upon?

_____

_____

_____

_____

_____

_____

_____

_____

_____

Observe the ways you multitask during the day and list those
situations and tasks.

Choose one task from the above list and simply focus
on that task. Describe your experience.

What do you value most in your life now?

_____

Have your values shifted over time, and in what ways?

_____

What is your greatest hope about change, in both yourself
and the world?

_____

What is your greatest fear about change, in both yourself
and the world?

_____

Describe how a family member sees you.

_____

Describe how a close friend sees you.

_____

Describe how an acquaintance sees you.

_____

Describe how a colleague or classmate sees you.

_____

Note the similarities or differences in the ways others see you (pp. 43-44).

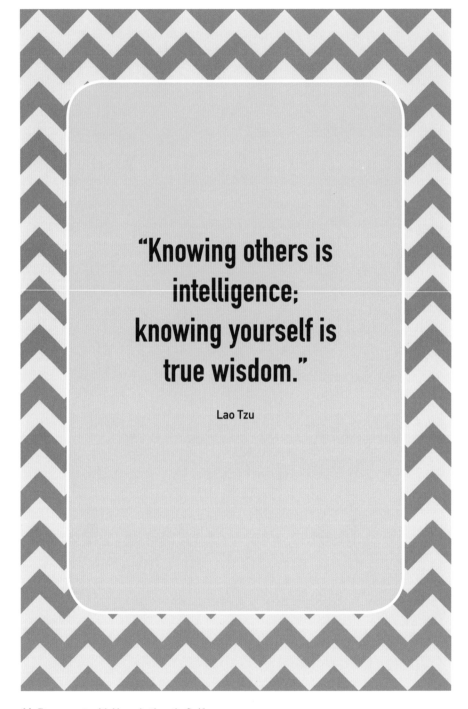

"Knowing others is
intelligence;
knowing yourself is
true wisdom."

Lao Tzu

Name five things you appreciate about yourself.

1

2

3

4

5

Name five things you appreciate about your best friend.

1

2

3

4

5

Describe yourself addressing a recent difficult situation and how you handled any strong emotions that came up.

Make a list of your unique strengths.

_____

What challenges do you face now, and which of your unique
strengths are supporting you?

_____

How do you make fun a part of your day at work or school
or while pursuing your goals?

_____

In what ways does your daily routine affect your habits
and vice versa?

_____

Do you wish you had more time each day?
What would you do in those extra hours?

_____

If you had an extra day each week to connect and
contribute to your local community, what would
happen during that bonus day?

_____

In what ways are you most flexible? List the pros and cons.

Pros	Cons

In what ways are you most rigid? List the pros and cons.

Pros	Cons

Who has the greatest impact on your life presently and why?

_____

_____

_____

_____

_____

_____

_____

_____

_____

How do the opinions of others, both useful and not useful,
affect your choices?

_____

_____

_____

_____

_____

_____

_____

_____

_____

Write a letter to your present self and express the ideas, principles, and excitement you have about your larger purpose in life. Include words of encouragement and inspiration that will be helpful as you face the challenges of change, both expected and unexpected.

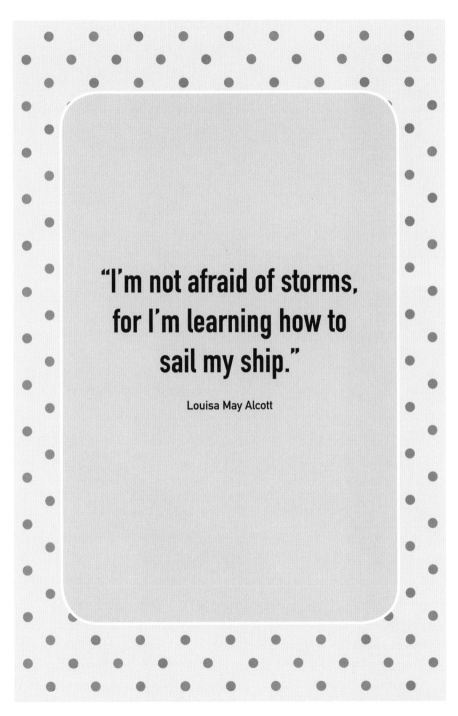

"I'm not afraid of storms,
for I'm learning how to
sail my ship."

Louisa May Alcott

3

DARE TO DREAM

Get inspired as you identify and expand
upon your ideas

Name 5 things you find beautiful today.

1

2

3

4

5

Name one thing, however small, you could do to create
positive change in the world today.

Which school subject do you wish you had studied when you were younger? How could you pursue that now?

Which community activity or event do you wish you had participated in when you were younger? How could you pursue that now?

Create an inventory of your expertise
and particular skills.

_____

TIP

Consider the areas
of knowledge people
often ask you about
when they're seeking
guidance, or things
that you're good at
doing for which
people come to you
specifically in order
to get the task done.

In what ways could you use these skills to contribute to a
community cause that you would be thrilled to be a part of?

_____

What is a new skill or skills you'd like to acquire and why?

How could you apply this knowledge to your future vision?

Make a list of any self-limiting beliefs that come up at times
of self-doubt. Next to each one list an empowering belief to
redirect your inner voice to convey confidence.

Self-limiting beliefs	Empowering beliefs

How do you envision success in your life?

"I attribute my success to this:
I never gave or took any excuse."

Florence Nightingale

How effective is your decision-making process? Consider which type of decisions are more difficult for you to make and which ones you find easier.

_____

List ways you could make better choices for yourself.

_____

Describe a favorable experience when you
responded spontaneously.

_____

Describe a favorable experience when you responded by
taking your time to plan.

_____

"To be is to do."

Immanuel Kant

In what ways do you, or could you, think outside the box when presented with a new challenge or changing circumstance?

_____

Bring to mind someone you think highly of. Which of their qualities would you like to emulate?

_____

Make a list of images and music or sounds that represent
and inspire courage, strength, confidence, resilience,
and creativity for you.

_____

....

....

....

....

....

....

....

....

....

....

....

....

....

....

....

....

....

....

....

NEXT STEP

Create a collage of the images or a playlist of the music or
sounds so you have visual or audio inspiration.

List three challenges in your life you've overcome and three challenges in your present life you'd like to take on.

Past challenges

1

2

3

New challenges

1

2

3

Create a list of current events and causes that
pique your interest.

_____

In what ways could you get involved in these areas in your
local community?

_____

Imagine you've received a substantial grant from an organization you greatly admire. Which organization is this? How much is the grant? Describe your cause, how you will use this funding, and who will benefit. Include the people on your dream team with whom you will collaborate and who will be excited to support your vision.

Describe an imaginary dinner with a famous person
you admire.

_____

Make a list of rebellious people you admire and why.

_____

If you could choose anyone in the world to be your life mentor, who would that be and why?

If you could choose anyone you know personally or in your local community to be your life mentor, who would that be and why?

Choose someone from your personal life and describe how
they are different from you.

Choose someone you don't know personally—someone you've
observed at a distance or only read about or watched in a movie.
Describe how they are different from you.

NEXT STEP

For both prompts on
this page, consider
how to accept and
embrace these
differences.

Name a world leader of today that you identify with most closely. What qualities in them do you respect?

If you could have a conversation with one of your ancestors, what would you ask them and how would you describe your life and your vision for the future to them?

Complete the following sentence in relation to a future dream
you have: "I can't wait until..."

_____

List three ways to bring your originality to the above
future dream.

_____

1

2

3

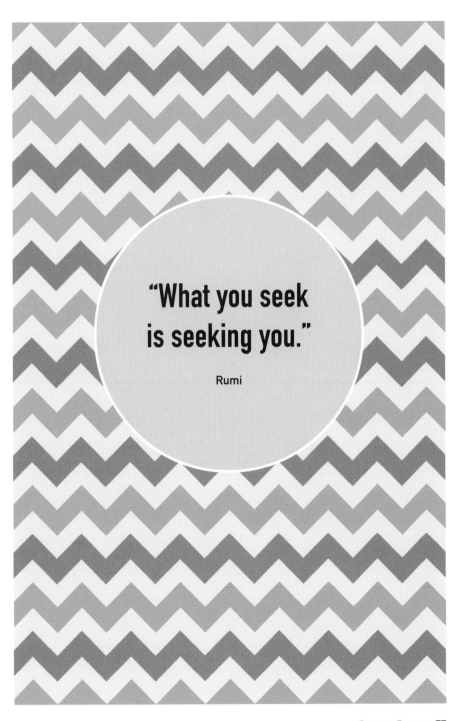

"What you seek
is seeking you."

Rumi

4

TAKE THE DEEP DIVE

Bring vision and action out into the
greater community

Say hello to one new person today and introduce yourself.
Describe the experience.

_____

What areas of your expertise and passion can you share with
others? Refer to your list of unique strengths (page 49).

_____

NEXT STEP

**Can you offer to mentor someone, either in your local
community or online?**

List three ways you can boost your confidence before
approaching new or challenging situations today.
Describe the outcome.

1

2

3

Outcome

What relationships in your life that are aligned with your
values would you like to enhance and how can you go about
doing so? List a few first steps to take.

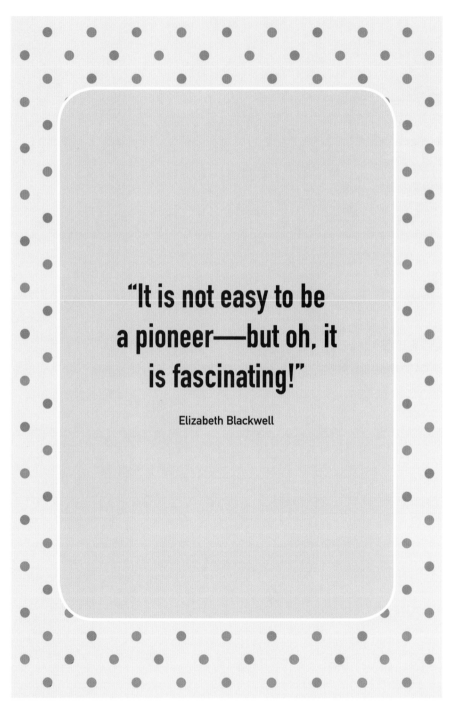

"It is not easy to be
a pioneer—but oh, it
is fascinating!"

Elizabeth Blackwell

What causes do you feel the urge to speak up about and why?

_____

NEXT STEP

Choose one cause from the above, decide on the best
platform to share your ideas with others—perhaps in a blog,
on social media, or at a community meeting—
and get started on it this week.

Provide a mission statement for a project you would like
to begin working on.

Make a pros and cons list for the above project. For example,
whether it is timely, the feasibility, your motivation, resources
you'll need, and a realistic time to launch.

Pros	Cons

In what ways could you use technology effectively and responsibly to support your project?

_____

_____

_____

_____

_____

_____

_____

_____

_____

_____

_____

Name three people you would like to collaborate with on this project.

_____

1 _____

2 _____

3 _____

NEXT STEP
Contact the people on your list this month to discuss further.

Would a lack of finances get in the way of your project?
List the steps you could take to improve that situation in
order of easiest to most challenging.

NEXT STEP

Take step one today.

What action or actions can you take to broaden your perspective about different people and cultures in your local community or the world at large?

Choose one action from the above to take this week and write about how the experience affected you.

Consider a person or persons in your neighborhood you only talk to briefly in passing. When appropriate, decide to expand the conversation to learn more about them and to share information about yourself, and mention your ideas regarding the community. Describe the experience.

TIP

By approaching someone you don't know so well, you may discover a new bond is created for future brainstorming or even for a project you can work on together.

"If you look the right way, you can see that the whole world is a garden."

Frances Hodgson Burnett

Describe a situation where you have been in opposition to another's beliefs, decisions, or choices. How did you respond?

_____

Was your response effective in a positive way? How so? If not, how could you have expressed yourself differently?

_____

TIP
Consider if your words are an improvement over silence. Listening to others and to your inner voice is important. So is what you say and how you say it to stay open and continue a conversation for greater understanding.

Refer to your collage of empowering and uplifting words on page 23. Choose one word to focus on, think about, and use in conversation and writing throughout the day. How did it affect your interactions with others and yourself?

_____

Continue the above exercise for two more days in a row, choosing a different word for each day. Record your observations here. Notice any changes in your interactions from day one to day three of this activity.

_____

Name the unmet needs in your community and opportunities
for growth and connection that are going unrecognized.

_____

Choose one of the above areas you'd love to get
involved with. Write up a brief plan of action to get this
started in your community.

_____

Envision the celebration that marks the first-year anniversary of your community effort or organization. Describe the details of the actual event, including your cause and mission statement, the people involved, and the yearly accomplishments and goals met.

You have been chosen to be the guest speaker at a ceremony for the graduating class of the high school you attended. The topic of your talk is: The key to making changes that work and lessons I've learned along the way. What are the main points of your speech? Include a closing inspiration for the students and faculty.

"Don't wait. The time will never be just right."

Mark Twain

5

SAY YES TO YOUR BEST SELF

Pay attention to self-care to support
your larger purpose

Describe what self-care means for you and how it is included
in your daily life now.

_____

Which of the above approaches are working for you,
and which ones aren't?

_____

Make note of any new approaches you'd like to explore further. Commit to at least one this week.

_____

Give yourself room to breathe. For a day, pay close attention to your breathing patterns. Describe your experiences here.

TIP

Focusing on your breath is helpful in finding calm, focus, and trust in the present. The simple breathing practice of "inhale confidence and exhale doubt" goes a long way.

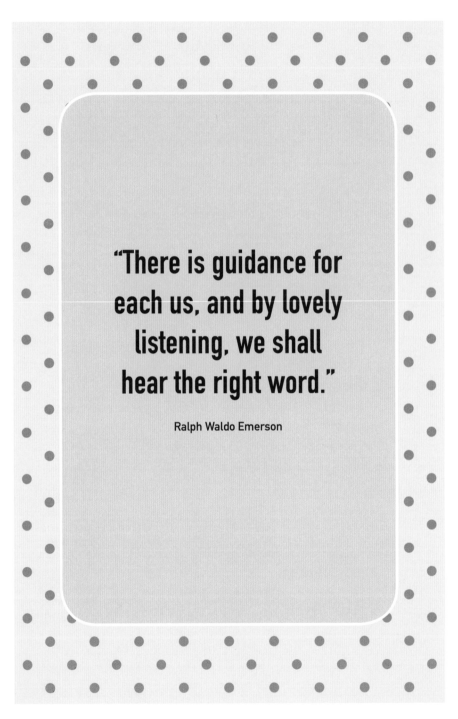

"There is guidance for each us, and by lovely listening, we shall hear the right word."

Ralph Waldo Emerson

List the supportive ways you connect with your true self.

Are you listening to what your mind, body, and heart are asking for? In what ways do you and can you answer that call to provide the needed attention and comfort?

Where are the places you go when relaxation or a time-out
is needed and why? How often is this included in your
daily routine?

_____

When was the last time you took a vacation?
Where did you go, how long were you away for,
and who were the people you traveled with?

_____

In what ways are you responsible for others in your life?

_____

Write about what's working and what's not in these areas
of your life and how you might prioritize better to pursue
your future dreams.

_____

Do you include meditation practice in your life? Describe your experience. If you're new to meditation, commit to exploring available options and testing the waters. Record what unfolds here.

TIP

Mindful meditation can calm your anxious mind to become focused and clear about what truly matters for you.

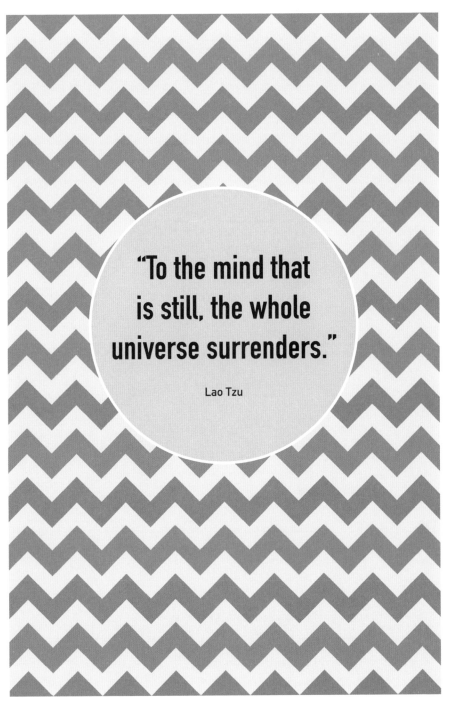

"To the mind that is still, the whole universe surrenders."

Lao Tzu

List all the activities you find energizing. This list is personal so only include what truly works for you, not what you think you should do.

TIP

Energizing activities may include being outdoors, movement, listening to music, cooking, meditation, daydreaming, creativity, or other hobbies you love.

Make a list of energizing activities or interests you're
curious to try out. Experiment with these options and
keep track of them here.

Make space for your dreams. What do you need to let go of in
your home to create more room, both physically and mentally,
to move more freely toward your vision of what lies ahead?

"Take rest: a field that
has rested gives
a beautiful crop."

Ovid

On average, how many hours do you sleep each night?
Do you feel well-rested the next day? Describe your typical
evening routine.

_____

List any ways to improve upon the above to ensure
better care for yourself.

_____

Your food choices can change you and the world. Are they supporting you to function at your best? Are they contributing to a sustainable and just world? List a few changes you'd like to make, however small.

_____

Financial wellness is an essential element of self-care.
Describe the current state of your personal finances.
Note any areas that are of concern and possible solutions.

_____

How does your personal financial situation affect the pursuit
of your larger purpose?

_____

In what ways can you increase your financial knowledge
to maintain a positive balance between all your interests
for now and beyond?

_____

View life in multicolor. Assign one or more of your positive
character traits to each color of the rainbow below.

Red

Orange

Yellow

Green

Blue

Indigo

Violet

In what ways do you or can you incorporate the colors on the opposite page in your living space and in how you dress?

_____

TIP

Assigning positive associations to colors and then consciously including them in your life can serve as an uplifting reminder.

Pay attention to your posture and body language throughout the day. Describe how you present yourself in different situations.

_____

Tune into how you feel when speaking about your idea or project to a new person. What's your comfort level and is your communication style effective? Describe a recent situation.

_____

Taking the best care of yourself includes discernment,
confidence and resilience. List the ways you do or
can expand upon these qualities.

You are your own kind of beautiful. In what ways do
you astonish yourself?

Setting intentions each morning for how you envision your day will support your present and future goals. List a few intentions that have meaning for you. Set this in motion for one week. Keep track of your experiences here and continue to add to your list.

Day 1

Day 2

Day 3

Day 4

Day 5

Day 6

Day 7

At the close of day, it is helpful to take time for a review of your day—what worked for you, what didn't, what to reconsider, how better to approach the following day. Set this in motion for one week. Keep track of your experiences here.

Day 1

Day 2

Day 3

Day 4

Day 5

Day 6

Day 7

In what ways do you follow your joy?

_____

What impact does the above have on your journey toward
a larger purpose in life?

_____

"We never know how high
we are till we are called to
rise; and then, if we are
true to plan, our statures
touch the skies."

Emily Dickinson

6

BE THE CHANGE AND REMAIN INSPIRED

Deepen your commitment to transforming

your present life and beyond

What represents freedom for you in your present life?

How does freedom factor into your vision of the future
and larger purpose?

How do your strengths empower you to change things both in your life and in the lives of others and your community, now and in the future?

_____

In what ways do you lead by example on a consistent basis?

_____

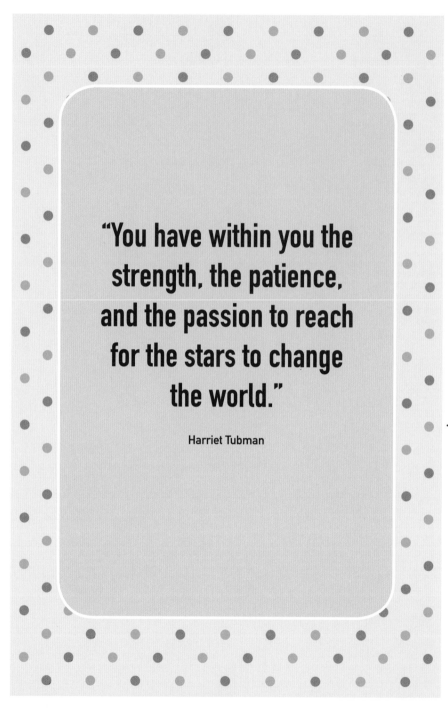

"You have within you the strength, the patience, and the passion to reach for the stars to change the world."

Harriet Tubman

Name three things you find hopeful today and
share with another person. Who did you choose to tell
and how did they respond?

1

2

3

Outcome

Identify three personal acts of courage from your week and
share with another person. Who did you choose to tell
and how did they respond?

1

2

3

Outcome

Do you surround yourself with people seeking greater meaning in life? Who are they and what are their pursuits?

_____

How do your most immediate relationships reflect your attitudes toward a life well-lived? Who brings out the best in you and who do you bring out the best in?

_____

As you move through your day, notice the ways to practice finding common ground with others. How did you connect more authentically, promote more cooperation, or remember to see the bigger picture?

NEXT STEP

Find a connection you have with others to a common purpose or vision and create a sense of belonging either locally or online. Perhaps begin by hosting a story circle for people to share life-changing stories. Who will you invite? Set a date for your first meet-up.

Select five favorite inspirational books on your bookshelf.
In what ways have they had an impact on your life story?

1

2

3

4

5

NEXT STEP

Consider hosting an inspirational book club in your local
community or online. List the steps to get this started, who
you will invite, and the first book selection for the group to
read and discuss.

"Once you make a decision,
the universe conspires
to make it happen."

Ralph Waldo Emerson

Make a list of positive actions you are taking now
and ones you plan to take in the future that are aligned
with your vision of change.

For one month, each week commit to one action from your list
of positive actions on the page opposite. At the end of the
month review the actions you took each week and note the
impact on your life, community, and future vision.

Explore untapped, hidden resources that could further
support your current and future plans. Make a list of ideas.

_____

Choose three of the above ideas to put into action this week.
Keep track of the outcome of your three actions here.

_____

1

2

3

Name a person you have lost touch with that you'd like to
reach out to again and say what would you like to ask them
in reference to your future vision.

Participate in a local youth mentoring program. What areas of
your knowledge and passion are you sharing with this future
generation? What are you learning from them in the process?

"The most effective way to do it, is to do it."

Amelia Earhart

Share knowledge with your peers. What expertise are you offering and in what ways are you seeking and/or building networks to connect with and support others in your area of interest?

Make a list of the networks you would like to join and/or organize.

NEXT STEP

Contact at least one network today. Keep track of your progress as you go down the list.

Take responsibility and give voice to your vision each day.
Create a list of ways you can pay it forward, however
small the action.

This week choose one action from the above list. Keep
track of your progress here, including the date you plan
to carry it out.

Unplug completely from your digital devices in two different conversations this week and replace with face to face contact. Who were your conversations with, what did you talk about, and did you note any differences in the way you shared and connected?

_____

_____

_____

_____

_____

_____

_____

_____

_____

_____

_____

_____

_____

_____

NEXT STEP

Repeat the above activity again next week, but this time, your conversations should pertain specifically to a new community idea or effort you would like to pursue.

Give yourself a ten-day challenge to focus on one vision, dream, or cause you'd like to bring out into the world. Create a one-sentence intention to describe it and repeat this intention to yourself each morning and evening for ten days. Keep track of your experience here and note any unexpected surprises that may arise during or after the ten days. Repeat the challenge in a month.

"At first people refuse to believe that a strange new thing can be done, then they begin to hope it can be done, then they see it can be done—then it is done and all the world wonders why it was not done centuries ago."

Frances Hodgson Burnett

Add a closing inspirational quote or uplifting image to your texts and emails. Begin doing this today. List ten ideas here to get started and keep adding on to it.

1

2

3

4

5

6

7

8

9

10

Further ideas

Write about three people you know very well that you are grateful for and why.

1

2

3

Write about three people you don't know very well that you are grateful for and why.

1

2

3

Take the time to thank three people in a special way
this month. Create a list of the different ways you will do
this and when it will happen.

NEXT STEP
Repeat again next month with three new people.

What will your legacy be?

"Light tomorrow
with today."

Elizabeth Barrett Browning